THE MAN ON THE MOON
Poems

Weeping World by Robert Bordo, 1986

THE MAN
ON THE MOON

POEMS

WILLIAM ALLEN

 NEW YORK UNIVERSITY PRESS
New York and London

Library of Congress Cataloging-in-Publication Data

Allen, William, 1957–
   The man on the moon.

  I. Title.
PS3551.L438M35 1987   811'.54   87-1705
ISBN 0-8147-0588-X

Book designed by Laiying Chong.

for
B. Westermann
and
L. de la Cruz Keil

CONTENTS

ACKNOWLEDGMENTS

Thanks to the editors of the publications in which the following
poems appeared:
lo Spazio Humano—"The City of Wooden Saints," "Departure"
Permafrost—"A Crucifixion"
The Blue Ox Review—"Willow"
The Dickinson Review—"Bluefish," "Haircut"
The Minetta Review—"A Crucifixion"

"Weeping World," drawing by Robert Bordo, 1986

I THE LOON

MILK

Where it all comes from,
the buckets and buckets of blood
to make this milk, first
cold, then boiling over,
a mother's milk, the cow's life
and the butcher barn,
the last factory of milk-making,
reaching out to Jews,
Muslims, the milk devourers
of the twenty-first century,
or the milk of the moon,
tipping out into your lap,
the ambrosia milk
of your sea-blue eyes, Love:
I soak you up
and drink you all in.

HAIRCUT

I wanted to be Frieda Kahlo,
sitting among her shorn locks of long black hair,
in long men's pants and wild with anger
at the hospitals in Chicago, and the meandering
path of the Mexican Revolution.
Diego had left her again, and here,
in this barber shop, I wanted to peel off
all my dirty clothes, give up peering
into neighbors' kitchen windows,
sleep for a century in a dark room
full of feather-light fossil moths.
I looked up into the mirror,
saw Campanella the barber as he whisked off
huge swaths of unmanaged hair, saying,
"Don't worry, I know what I'm doing."
An electric haircutter was whirring over
my head, my ears, fluffing off
the topmost layers.
It was the horrible machine that Mom had used
when we were small, reducing us
to shaven images of little American doughboys.

Next to me, the scissors snipped away
at the eyebrows of a cook's fine grey hair,
as another man sat, rocked his crossed legs,
immersed in pictures of nude Madonna.
I look at myself in the mirror,
see the small black speck in one eye,
sink back into the chair as this man's hands
encircle my warm skull, and I feel again
the priest's wandering fingers,
holding the sides of my head together,
whispering some unbelievable catechism.
I feel my mother's firm soft bosom
pressed close to my face, as she snips
and shaves, and my sister's shape
tight against mine, or the hard heartbeat
of the woman who has just left me to cry
in the arms of an unfamiliar barber.
Outside, in broad daylight on Broadway,
ladies' undergarments on hangers shoot down
wire lanyards from trucks into cellar doors,
as shoppers and *operadores* peer inside
at the boy in the chair, as they run
to lunch of rice and beans at *La Perla*.
But I see the stubs of coarse white hair,
know she won't be the last to leave me.
Campanella holds a mirror behind,
picks out lotions for the finishing touch,
wildroot, witch hazel, and barbicides,
water and talc and cream for shaving,
and the long thin straight edge
which scrapes a clean line along my neck.
The razor delicately traces the circle

5

of the ears, redefines
the frown on my forehead.
I think of Frieda again, how she kept painting
in spite of herself, never lost the courage
to articulate the tiny, inorganic things
that made their way into her bathtub.
I gather the strength to thank Campanella,
put on my overcoat and dash back out
into the brisk October air, breathe deep,
my hairs already starting to grow back.

DIANA

Diana was bathing in a forest stream,
her beautiful handmaidens carefully washing
under her arms, her legs, the delicate
spot behind her neck.
A hunter came upon them, having lost his way,
and from a distance, he secretly watched
as the goddess spread out her arms
in the warm sun.
She felt his presence, saw him there behind a tree.
Angrily, she turned and looked into his eyes,
until he couldn't move or feel his legs
or make them run away.
Antlers sprouted from his head,
then tufts of hair on his arms thickened, the ankles
bent and drew themselves out,
toenails smoothing into hooves, and his nose
lengthened into the muzzle of a snout.
When he cried out, the deep-throated man sounded
a voiceless bleat, and he fled in fear of this,
his hunting dogs close at his feet,
catching the unfamiliar scent.

The largest of them sunk his teeth
into the soft hide, the undulating vertebra,
and quickly felled this stag,
so unused to running on four legs.
The rest of the pack came up, bit into his neck,
knees, throat, the flesh of his heavy head.
The woods became silent.

We crossed the sound on a ferry,
landing gently at a crossroads in Orient Point.
From there we drove another several miles,
to my mother's friend whom no one had seen
or heard from for twenty years.
She had a small green house with shutters
and a wide porch, with room enough underneath
for chickens or pigs.
Inside, linoleum floors and flowered curtains,
talk of divorces and one small daughter
who didn't like other children,
in any town they'd moved to.
I wandered with my brothers, then upstairs alone,
suddenly faced with a strange woman
who stared fiercely into a mirror.
Her shirt was off, hanging on the sink,
and her hair was tangled wildly.
I couldn't look away, and she stared at me
through the mirror, until I felt my legs
were turning into stones.
My mother called, her friend Merlie was crying,
a sad bloodhound sat on the back steps.
As we drove off, my sister said that Diana
was insane, from her mother and LSD,

but what I knew was that I saw something
I wasn't meant to see: the wild look,
and my wide eyes looking back at her reflection,
her nakedness assaulting me.
The rest of the trip I was quiet,
staring inward into the leather of the seat.
The sea was restless on the return crossing.

GASPARD DE LA NUIT

Listening to this,
I think of a hand of seven fingers,
a wall of sun-bent glass,
a boy, playing in the bricks
of a fallen cathedral
in downtrodden Palermo.
I remember a poem I once wrote
to you before I knew you,
of an angry sea
and a rich tide which quelled its fire.
A moon ago, stranded on a river,
I saw the boy, the glass,
the bricks, your smile again.
Tonight I welcome the darkness
which hides its face
in your mother's arms.

WATCHING THE CHALLENGER AT COLUMBUS SCHOOL

How I hate the television now.
The lift-off looked perfect, and the sky
was cold and blue.
The TV was huge, and the ground crew
assumed their normal tones of voice, until
a striding, striding,
as they went for full throttle,
before anyone could say or see a thing,
Phoo! into a million pieces
and white tails of smoke trailing off,
just as the shuttle went from clear blue
to what seemed to be the blackness
of space, the moment of interface.
Rocket boosters bursting into soundlessness.
The newsman was crying—no one
was saying anything, as they usually do.
"I'm just too shocked," he kept
repeating, the vapors shooting down,
and I imagined the footbones,
thermometers, and wreckages of fusilage

floating down to the Indian Ocean.
There was nothing.
Did they reach to touch the face of God
before they died? The sky
was the most beautiful of blues,
and all around the room,
the teachers were horrified:
they had lost one of their own.
But the children saw nothing new,
as if the sequel to *Airplane II*
came on a little early in the day.
Until one child saw the principal
wiping tears, and then she asked
"Are they really dead?"
The kids didn't get it, the television
had cried *Wolf* too many times before,
and now these boys and girls
would grow up without the sense,
the sense that I still feel, to take
a sledgehammer and go around the world
to every set and smash it
into bits before it's way too late.

STONY CREEK

From out of the steel cot that I share
with a brother I've beaten blue,
I hurry to the kitchen in search of water
or a light to chase away the shadows
which frighten me.
The cold goes into my feet as I try to walk
lightly across the stone floor.

Somebody is crying in the other room:
it sounds like a goat, stuck in a snake's throat.
I've never heard this sound before, my father
choking on his own tears while his children
pretend to be sleeping.
I didn't know who he was or why we were here,
in this flat which shook when trains went by.

Sitting low to the table in my underpants,
I thought about Mom and our house by the river,
magpies angrily vying for position
in maple trees by the gravel driveway.
I remember the day he came there, to take us

to the beach, and while we hid under beds
Mom threw rocks at his car.

In the afternoon, John had put a penny
on the railroad tracks, flattened into one
of those wafers for the tongue on Sundays.
In the woods, we found a pit of anthracite,
no miners or shovels or blasting caps,
and Dad said nothing about where the coal went.
He didn't talk at all, but he was with us.

At the cove below, we shot rocks into the waves,
watched fishermen as they swore at women
and inched their nets into a lobster boat.
Among the scraps and waste of bait,
an old male cat was nursing an open wound.
Dad gazed out past the creek,
the crippled shore, to where the ospreys lived.

Back in bed, warmth returns to my hands and feet
as Ted puts his arms around me, smiles in his sleep.
In the dark, Dad gets up, headed for his job
at the women's prison, covers his pale
overworked body with a thin green suit, carries
out the garbage and closes the back door,
as the Erie Lackawanna rocks through Stony Creek.

RENDEZVOUS IN MOUNDSVILLE

We spoke briefly on the phone
some battered voices interrupting us
as we talked about our spouses,
how they were out and how we could meet
after your return from the Sudan,
from the desert nomads and their crops
on fire and wars and endless
walkings to the river.
How we might meet halfway between
our complicated lives, to spend a night
and look again into each other's eyes.
I gave up on the ruler, finding
no straight roads and an overwhelming
impulse to measure across Lake Erie,
instead of around it, thinking that
maybe we could go as crows.
I thought of how Magellan must have
done it, finally closed his eyes
and pointed down the straits
of South America, the Tierra del Fuego
and the hurricane capes of fear.

My finger trembled, came down
between the states between us, as I'd
once come down by you at night,
not in the woods you'd dreamed us to,
but to the banks of the Ohio River,
not far from Wheeling, West Virginia
and James Wright's long nights of
sweating out his driven love for everything
that was dirty or wasted or broken.
In Moundsville, no, a little bit
below it, at the mound itself.
Serpentine curves and temple hillocks,
the furrows would cry in the voices
of animals whose spirits lived inside.
We'd not get there together,
you, in your farmer pickup truck,
the front of which is smashed with bugs
from potholed roads streaming out
of Detroit, and me, on the early
morning Greyhound through Pittsburgh,
packed with nuns and iron workers
on their way to temporary jobs in Dayton.
No one would be there by the mound.
Even the muskrats, worshipped by
the architects of this primeval
burial ground, would be asleep
in the sun above the marsh holes
on mini-islands of the creeks.
Your breath would be vaporous,
and the river running full, coldest
waters pushing down to the bayous.
We'd walk as nomads to the western bank,

bathe ourselves and look up at the moon
rising over a forest of chestnut trees.
Small new stars would be twinkling,
alive with origins quite apart from
yours or mine. We'd drive the dirt road
back to Moundsville, to the warmest
blue motel of cabins where we'd make
a fire and bless our food, watch the owl's
eye andirons as they heat from red to white.
And sit and talk and touch again.
I'd say I felt as if we'd already made love,
and again you might not understand. But
this time I'd be right. And the glimmering
eyes of the owls would darken slightly,
go back through red to ashen gray,
and softly then not glow at all.

BLUEFISH

It was the night they bombed Cambodia.
Grandaddy was screaming at Mom
with a red face
and fish on the table.
Would we impeach him?
They tried to make us eat.
His bald head was glistening
like Nixon's lips—
he knew for whom she had voted,
a carving knife in his hand.
I looked down at the plastic
tablecloth covering lace.
They drank sherry, watched Lawrence Welk
when we wanted to see *The Birds*.
We had to eat his hard-boiled eggs
every morning, the five of us
sleeping on their fireplace rug.
And she made their son unhappy,
speaking her mind about things
that shouldn't concern her.
He was a navigator, pharmaceutical

sales wiz, Dale Carnegie guest lecturer,
French tutor to pretty ladies.
And every night he'd draw out the tiny lines
on red graphs of his little stocks.
He'd built his own speedboat out of wood,
fishing the shoals off Point Judith,
Oak Bluffs, Horseneck Beach, L'Hommedieu.
He wanted us to come along happily,
huddled by the fish bucket
and extra can of gas as he pounded
through the ten-foot waves
with his Evinrude 80 and his pale
fragile smiling wife clenching the compass.
We were in ridiculous life jackets
and long-brimmed visors,
spray in our faces.
I was sick to my stomach every time,
broken-jawed fish staring up at me
from the drainage pit of the engine.
I wondered if I hated him.
He never looked me in the eye:
only *he* was allowed to cut the meat or fish.
I sat there chewing and chewing
the night Mom ran out of his house
in tears, knowing I'd never swallow it.

THE POETRY READING

Every night he'd read for hours
from Dickens, Tennyson, Whittier, or Kipling.
It was painful, all the heavy rhyming
and rumpling of the language,
the facile notions of world and man and genocide.
He asked his son, my father, once,
what he thought of my poems, and Dad replied
he really didn't know, a man who always
got excited by my news of working on cars
or painting boats, but never by what
I was writing or thinking or feeling.
This night, in his cool and well-protected house
in Riviera Beach, he'd read some
epic poem about Alaska Joe and his buxom bride.
I went to bed with cramps, and my wife
told me to fight fire with fire, so we planned
a gala reading for the next night.
I had to make him listen, learn about my life.
He fought in the war in Italy, lost everything
in the Depression, lived in a city boardinghouse
apart from his wife and sons in the country.

He didn't want to know the underside
of living, but only of the happy things,
a phrase I never understood.
He'd never heard of Lowell's nephew, once
or twice removed, a man who grasped
something of the world I sought to comprehend.
I started with something pleasant,
a desert landscape, or birds and beasts at play,
but right away I saw him tip back
in his Craftmatic chair and start to sleep
as I read on, louder, knowing he was hard
of hearing, that he didn't want to listen.
There was no familiar ring to bind a line
to the next, no pontifical odes to princesses,
no jerky iambics or great white hopes unchallenged,
no brilliant or manifest destinies.

A gecko then unhooked its claw from a drape
and skittered down onto the lime-green floor.
He kept glancing at his watch.
My grandmother Tippet listened intently,
and for all her pleasantries and sheltered life
I think she understood—no, felt, what I read.
Then, out of the blue of his Floridian paradise,
he flicked on the tube by remote control,
routed the channel knob to seven, just
as Wisk detergent gave way to the titles
for an animated *Tale of Two Cities.*
I was too shocked to speak, never more hurt
in all my life, right in the middle of a story
about my father, how sad and broken up
he was to live alone after leaving his wife.

Tippet looked on sympathetically,
seemed to say, *Don't blame him,
he sees with other eyes.*
And I couldn't, as I thought of his supreme
devotion to his boys, his pure belief
in the myth of the birth of the hero,
how he shaped his life completely out of dust,
how much he gave to me with his flamboyant, masterly
readings of the classics, how proud he was
to memorize the poems his father read to him,
not to mention modern ones, like *Casey at the Bat,*
even its latter half which he confessed was hard
because it didn't follow logically.
And I thought of a letter he wrote to me,
back in my student days, where he spoke of the need
for fathers and sons to not agree,
of the many-sided world, each soul a separate
instrument in a symphony.
To my bass clarinet, he was the strumming ukelele
he later played for us, a serenade to his love
that made me weep, and then I knew,
in some small way, that he was also right,
and that, despite it all, I loved him very much.

THE LOON

It was an immaculate conception.
We were both thirteen.
I couldn't sleep for the pounding
in my head, and thought about the loon
I'd been watching earlier that day.
He was diving for scup in the bay,
one time dove down without coming up.
I counted and counted, held my own breath
to see if I could match his time.
Minutes went by, he didn't reemerge.
Could a bird become a fish?
As I lay in bed, I thought it over,
knew what I had to do: get up
and go to her, with some excuse,
a goodnight kiss perhaps.
I wanted to feel her breasts, her breath,
and move my hand down slowly to where
it had never been before.
So I walked through shadows
and entered her room, placed a kiss
upon her cheek, expecting her or someone else
to do the rest.

I said that I wanted to hear her heart beat,
that I had to feel it with my hand.
I pulled aside the cover, crept inside
the bed while she said nothing
as if sleeping or even dead.
My hand went to hers, and then I felt
her heart at work, and the delicate hardening
of a nipple above it, the touch of some
angelic mouth which caused the bump to swell
and rise under my caress.
She was as scared as I, stayed motionless.
And then my hand moved down, the way my plan
had instructed, to reach at last beneath
her navel, the first fine wisp of hair
where I stopped and burrowed in
for what seemed to be hours.
I came to love the pulsing of my fingertips,
the stiff warm shell which now responded
to my awkward kisses at her mouth.
And then I left, and walked outside
and couldn't sleep and found the sea awake
which rose above its water marks
as a hurricane approached the island.
The moon shone down fully upon me:
I knew what I had done and what I didn't do.
For though I understood some things
a fear grew up inside of me, as I thought
of her father, how he beat his boys with sticks
if they stayed out too long.
What if somehow she was pregnant?
And something changed inside of me, as I sat
on boulders by the shore and thought

of what the world would do to our child.
Luminous snails cast up their light
to the gigantic moon over the waters.
The fear was growing into something else,
as I felt her heart still beating inside me.
I had a sudden urge to run away
or burn myself horribly with the spark of warmth
that she had given me, something that now
was mine. I walked past the decoy owl
who prowled the docks and kept the gulls
from shitting there, past the quahog beds
where we painted red lips onto clams,
past the mouth of the river which seemed
a huge womanly body that I could love now,
hold all of inside me, and the fear sank down
into some hidden spot, as my arms and legs
began to burn again, feel the cold sweat
of our lovemaking, deliver the child
which this night had given me.
Then, bright as fire under the huge storm moon,
I saw him there again, as he came up quick
with a wild and struggling river bass.
It was the loon! He had come up again!

II   INVISIBLE CITIES

PSALM

There is a field of goldenrod where
the bloody animal of dawn swallows
the sputum of the wood king's eyes.
I wake to the flycatcher's rasping,
and the silence of the hemlock's dew.
This is the last morning of waiting:
the dream of Joachim has clouded into
pollen in the air, and no woman
nor man can rise from bed without
knowing a special light, the delicate
fragrance which brings a messenger.
There are mountains behind this open
field, the path which leads into long,
scarred mouths of the Anti-Christ.
And there is the old grist mill where
farmers are buried in shadows
of grinding stones set firmly into
the fertile earth of this parish.
A small hand rises up out of the sea
of grass, extends to me the cup
which bears waters of a distant

river in Mauritania or Mali.
This is the day of forewarning,
the violent bearing away the violent,
the rich usurping the rich.
One of my hands is black from soil.
The wind sings a cold melody as we
embrace, and I look into your eyes,
the gray-green eyes of the lizard
who sits up and speaks in the grass.

COVENANT OF THE ARK

In the beginning was the black grackle:
and out of her eyes, the oily eggs of the masked piranha,
the seven granite peaks, a host of flowery
cinch-bugs, notched mouths of fire-eating bears,
and the purplish tail of the trogon.
As she flew towards light, her wings spun out
a fiercer wind to whip the sea
into a gold ocean of phosphorescent eels,
who calmed themselves and calmed the night
until it opened into mountains, the laughing ears
of a distant and rumbling volcano.
Out of her slim beak, as words shook their fists
and the rain fell down, a first song was born:
the mating call of whooping cranes,
the dry heaves of thunder from the North,
the lamb's incessant search for greener grass,
the last shriek of a rabbit, caught in the talons
of a bird of prey,
the whispering silicates and glacial walls,
the shy voices of deer at a watering hole.

After this long morning of wakening,
she ate and shat.
What came out was a man, fully clothed, stunk up
with gin, almost giggling as he sucked
the moisture out of frozen leaf-tips.
Where was the woman? Where did the bird fly off to?

DESERT MUSIC

I wake to small children crying.
Egypt is across the sea.
A boy is leading the others towards a boat
on a nearby shore.
Fishermen walk quietly to their nets:
some are already hungry.
One man readies the sails for a crossing.
Slaves watch and smile to each other.
A scroll is unfurled with a lesson,
a hieroglyphics of the moon.

The sea of sand is vast and unobtrusive.
We pick the last fruit, leave our enemies behind.
Olive trees bend in the wind,
and they cry as the doves of mercy,
the long, tired arms of Bedouins.

Flutes of bird leg bones
rise up out of the red-veined rocks
of this cold and desolate sierra.
Kids carry the wounded sheep on their backs,

the food and wine of this broken-hearted journey.
Someone has drunk of the frankincense,
and a woman plays a sad tune on the last flute.
We clean up the orchard before leaving.

THE FLOATING GARDENS OF XOCHIMILCO

A monkey scratches his head
in the thick jungle root,
as a red mawcaw stirs up the dusk
with plaintive cries:
the only smells are the green iguanas
hanging up by the roadsides.
Deep in the mangroves, boats
made of bark glide across the mist,
in the half-light of tiny islands
in a lost lake.
My lantern has gone out.
A leopard's eyes pick up a fine beam
of light from the moon, illuminate
the ancient black lagoon.
A woman on a funeral bier, full breasts,
almond eyes, trembles slightly
as the boat crosses an alligator's ripple.
The snakes and vines were climbing
into my arms as she opened her eyes,
and a child cried out for milk.

I should have been the sacrifice.
Would Tlaloc be proud?
There was something in me
that leaned towards disaster, towards
the people of the swamp
coming out to hang up their lizards
to sell to the tourists.

A LITANY FOR NIGHT

We love what we don't know
We kill unseen beasts
and scatter their bones over the earth
We use our hands to fool ourselves
We burn the mockingbird who eats her eggs
We kick at alley cats
or take them into our homes
We forget our Indian ancestries
and burnish the scars off the skin
We sneer at homeless men
or take them into airy tombs
We want to live in open mouths
or walk into the dark eyes of the dying
We watch the lake's shadow
and feel the ice freeze on city swamps
We lie down with wolves to understand ourselves
and save the fear of ghosts for thunderstorms
We wait for someone else to move the stone
or wait for wombs to break apart
or build us up again
or speak to us, of restless bodies in the sea

Tippet looked on sympathetically,
We take what we want
and want to bring alive the calmest waters
We watch for signs of laughter
in shaking hearts and open wounds
We find the doors are closed at night
and we love, sometimes,
to name the smaller things
like *bloodroot* and *meadow mice.*

SOCORRO, NEW MEXICO

for Carrie Yamaoka

Here is the landscape of your musical scores
and of you as a child in a picture.
Here is the occasional bison, and the blue-black
jackals who roam the empty parking lots.
Here are mounds of Tiwa ruins
and geodes from the first moon walk.
Here is dust and smoke from pueblo revolts
and heads of Anglos hanging on sticks.
Here is the empty swimming pool of the motel
where I lay and drank Coors tall boys
into morning, while whippoorwills sang of another
sort of life, far from iron ore and coffee shops
crowded with grandmothers and cowgirls—
of Etruscan swords and concentration camps,
ageless shells and animal humps
and the crumbling Rosebud Bar
where I drank to you and to the horses
you drew in foamy streams,
and to the yellowthroats dipping their yellow

in clover fields and Hopi dreams.
I wish you could hear the quavering voices
of the night which call out to you:

I am the old mule deer who feeds at dawn.
I am the giant saguaro that harbors the cactus owl.
I am the wind that beats down doors at night,
the desert's tears, which beckon a journey of death.
I am the tongue of the diamondback,
the antlered pronghorn's ghost who runs and runs and runs,
*   and always comes back again.*
I am the broad-winged eagles who soar and do not flap
their wings, after the prairie dogs are silent
and the giant spiders of the rye
have stuffed themselves.

THE BOSQUE DEL APACHE

(A bird sanctuary near the White Sands Missile Base, N.M.)

Turkey vultures land in the dead-limbed cottonwoods,
as white-tailed deer chase off a coyote—
some relative of Anubis—just as she squats
and pees into an arroyo.
The Rio Grande is closing up for the night,
and the sun goes down behind the hills of clay.
Twenty miles south, men shack up with army wives,
on long boy beds flown in from Chicago.
As they enter each other (the women make love
to the men), pheasants do their wooing
out on the plains, and mosquitos conquer the bogs,
the vultures shrug, sleepy owls begin their hunting.
We drive off the road to watch the mourning doves,
listen to the soft laments which bring us back
to this life-giving river, in which we try to see
ourselves, take back what we've taken away.
As the night comes out, I see that several satellites
are trying to look like stars.

ANGKOR WAT

How to approach the child without arms?

Terrified by the mortar rounds,
she crawls into the burnt body of an American Jeep.
I'm in there already, singing an old song
to an old man:
a prince of the forest pursues
the wicked, fire-breathing dragon.
A soul is bought, two bloodthirsty nights
he spends alone on a mountaintop,
and then . . . the old man's heart is failing.
The little girl wants to hear an end
to the story.
Over the sound of fire-bombs searing
into straw windows,
I tell her that the dragon and the prince
become friends, and live together
at the bottom of a beautiful black lake.

A CRUCIFIXION

Below in the dark, Veronica waits to wipe the face.
Thick-feathered eagles dust out their wings
and peck at tiny specks of bloodied meat.
Into the hot black holes of distant hills, forgotten
soldiers suck the last breath out of the daylight.
Villagers pound thick wooden stakes into the ground
as the black sky casts its shadow over heaven.

Hanging from crooked poles, the soft body tenderly
pulls at two thin wrists
and sags above the nail holes
in two bony feet.
Dark circles surround the closed lids:
there are no stars
to draw the last light out of his eyes.

A sleeping nighthawk stirs, opens his
giant, froglike mouth and croaks to God
about the spirit ascending into the fields of coal.
Veronica unwinds the linen shroud from about
his waist, and, naked now,
attends to the corrupted flesh.

MONDRIAN'S *PIER AND OCEAN*

1

The composition must be oval.
As the sky is round, and cirrus clouds
command the aesthetics of weather,
the storm will soon approach.
The symmetry of houses by the sea,
an idealization of the machine.
We cry for the unwed mothers.

2

And girls on the docks do the men's work
of hauling up the crates of oranges.
Tins of charcoal unattended,
day-old mackerel wrapped in Soviet newspaper.
Sailors sing in native French
about the bird who could not fly.
A wide gray horizon, the slap of wake
upon rocks, a gray-green sun slowly
going down beneath the ocean.

3

A symmetry in the wind.
Pier full of strangers, walking dogs
or with lovers to see the islands,
laughing gulls all headed into the blow,
and pots of fresh fish, Dutch flowers,
as the whole world turns
and gives the pier its last embrace.

4

Somebody is painting on the pier.
Ordering the yellows and the catboats
that yawn, the lyrical twining of windmills.
Windows without curtains,
no fingers in the dike.
Pale rose tulips and the mother cat
who walks her newborns out into the picture.
A womb or a fruit,
and dirty smelts lying on a boot
while under the boardwalk
the mayor's daughter puts her tongue
in a young man's mouth.
It isn't too late.
Skiffs and dories bounce as one wake
pounds into another.
Skimmers lace the breakers
and alter the swell.
Thimble islands tremble underneath.
The waves are deconstructive.

5

Cold winds of winter,
the heavy cranes will heave their muds
river-wise, smells of coffee and oil
will break the taste of salt.
An azure blue at the moment of dusk,
mermaids searching still
for those to trust.

6

The sea is the same as always,
and the giant squid will swim in it.
A submarine glides by silently,
men don't stop their fishing.
An ocean liner stands by
far out at sea; we don't know why
they're fighting in Japan and Germany.
A child picks at a blue crab claw
as the lighthouse booms its warning.

7

One wake still troubles another.
A ship-wrecked destroyer goes under.
Prothonotary warblers V-pattern the sky,
hasten the impending gray: a rain,
another day, a commitment to something.
The painter on the pier keeps painting.
The composition must be oval.

A LITTLE PRAYER FOR THE SOUL OF
THE WHITE ANT, OR FOR RAIN

The wind is the breath of a woman,
hot with the passion of night-blooming flowers.
A dog measures his steps to the cracked rim
of the riverbed: below, lungs racked
with sweat or spit, three lion cubs have drawn
their mouths into the open guts of a gazelle.
There is no echo in the rip and tearing of flesh.

A weaver bird twists a blade of grass
around the curvature of two supple twigs.
Up in the sky, yellowed by clouds or by dust,
a goose calls out its solitary name at dusk.

Submerged in tons of mud,
a hippopotamus farts out a week's worth
of oily weeds, while on the plains
beyond an ancient burying ground,
many dark men with faces painted white
sit together and carve at sticks from trees.

SARDINIAN MEADOW

It was the home of the orchid
that smelled like rotting meat.
Into these rocks, blood flies
would travel from all over,
allured by the stench of carrion.
Once down the fleshy throat
of the flower, caught in the trap
like trembling children praying
before their Christmas beds,
the flies could only drop down
singly into the sticky
sugared pool of yellowed water.
But a few would escape, having
laid their eggs instinctively
and wiped their backs against
the flecks of pollen, to make their
way to other plants of the same
imperfect perfume, prostrate
themselves before the fragrance,
sacrifice their freedom to this

monstrous need to eat of wasted,
rotting, animal flesh.

What was I doing there?
The smell of the dead was over-
whelming: the artichoke fields
were littered with the broken plants.
Someone was stamping them out,
the way we used to smash skunk cabbage
long ago, back in the Old Lyme swamps.
All around was barrel cactus,
strangely comfortable here
by the sea, and by the old
white tuna factory where boys would
first initiate themselves
into the hard and fast mysteries
of the carrion orchids.
But for these blossoming men
there was no need to sacrifice flies.
Nor was there a need for girls
and their loose-fitting skirts:
they were other deadly flowers,
ones not to be touched.
They would go into the windowless
mausoleum to find the deep secrets
of the abandoned canning rooms,

while I walked circles around the yard,
the small cemetery, the lonely spire
of rusted brick which met the sea.
What was a stormy petrel doing, flying
about the ravaged sands and rocky coast?

49

And where was the ghost of Antonio Gramsci—
lost, among the fat-tongued graves?
I thought about what he once told me,
how we are all just fertile cow shit
for somebody else's revolution,
the boys of this factory waiting to become
leaders or fighters or farm workers.
And this pure white Nordic bird
shining as if out of glass upon this
Mediterranean shore, what did she know
of the things I had come there to see?
How fragile we are, as we crawl on
hands and knees, slink back up into
the fleshy mouth of the flower without
thinking, every time it rains into
the dark wet throat of the orchid
which thrives in the Sardinian meadow.

STILL LIFE OF A BOY AND
FLYING FISH

C'est un plus petit coeur.

In a rock grotto on Andros,
he poses without any clothes, like Adonis
under towering clouds of autumn,
his shivering cock like a man's drawn out
by thoughts of sex or death
or the deepest maelstrom of the ocean.
He has the soft bloated belly of a leptosome,
a crooked back, skinny arms and hips,
the rose-red cheeks and drawn-back lips
of a recent bout of fervent kissing.
He has the black hair of an Arabian horse,
and the fierce dark eyebrows of Istanbul.
In his arms, he cradles a flying fish,
some kind of winged herring, wizened and dry
from lack of salt and underwater currents.
With his right hand he forms a claw
to balance the bony back and hold open

51

the paper-thin and poisoned wings, while
the fish with its puckered lizard mouth
and swollen eyes swallows whole
the index finger of his left hand.
Green sea poppers and tiny orange snails
cling to the mossy rock, where an iron ring
is set in jagged granite, just below
the boy's navel, the smaller heart, the center
of the picture, the last fingerhold
of a forgotten god, chained and mauled here
by an eagle. But this boy is free, and
he smiles the lascivious smile of Cassandra.

THE CITY OF WOODEN SAINTS

for Patricia Jones

Is this the city of love?
Where you smelled the cold of summer amarylis
and blind old men sold you white grapes
at the foot of Piazza Navona?

I remember how you said the blood ran calmly
out of the Tiber, into the park where lovers
hide behind benches and Hermaphrodite
lets herself nightly out of the museum.

In Santa Maria del Popolo, Paul still lies
under the heavy iron hoof, and beautiful men
in long black scarves gather in cafes
to carve up the dead partisans.

The horse head fountain is splashing
a puddle of water onto the Spanish steps.
Keats walks with tomcats in the belfry:
the pyramid of Cestius remains the center.

Rooftops catch the dying sun,
the brown of fading revolutions.
A body floats on the green river, past Castel
Sant'Angelo, the brigidisti, the carabinieri.

Apollo's lost his love to the blossoms of dusk.
Here is the ancient kiss of the catacombs.
The black sands of Ostia are far away.
It *is* the city of love.

CAPE FINISTERRE

for Charlotte Swiezinski

You walked the dun medieval paths
through France, the Pyrenees, the unnavigable
roads of western Spain, as others once
journeyed to Rome, the holy lands, through
pines and eucalyptus, to reach the oldest lighthouse
on the continent, the sullen guider of ships,
to hear in the shadow of his bones
the final words of James.
You came to live among the outcast Celts,
the stocky fishermen of blazing orange hair,
thick marsala wines, music of bagpipe,
scores of wives wailing into stormy nights,
tankers rolling onto shoals at sunrise.
You wanted to find a place to rest,
among the loud squawkers of the natural world,
far from the tongues of fire in Europe,
where even demons believed—and shuddered.
I see you on the high chalk cliffs,

looking out towards the place you left behind,
hearing in the winds what brought you there,
what will bring you back to us again,
Be doers of the word, not hearers only . . .

III THREE POEMS FOR
JANE DICKSON

ELDORADO

I imagine this long elegant
automobile to be pulled in to a corner
somewhere just above Times Square.
Has the driver gone off for Chinese food,
to buy some pornographic magazines,
or visit a tenant above the storefront
which has a sign, *Superfly?*
I don't know why I imagine the driver
is a longshoreman, or for that
matter, the male sex of the person
who stands against the wall, next
to the eerie green lamp of the bookstore.
In a fluorescent, hooded sweatshirt,
he must be some sort of arctic messenger.
Or is it a woman, waiting out a girlfriend
who pees in an alley behind the newstand?
How will I ever know what she is doing
there, or what she must be guarding?
I know—she must have something to do
with the car, the Eldorado.

RYDER'S ALLEY

Named for Albert Pinkham Ryder,
no doubt, who must have teetered down
Gold and Fulton full of rum,
having come from another session
for his *Death on a Pale White Horse,*
or another dark and restless
painting of the sea, like this night
in Ryder's Alley, where a man
holds himself open against
an overflowing dumpster, crammed full
of polyester floss, by the loading dock
of a nineteenth-century cardamom
shop, where I smell curries and feel
the rain finishing its downfall,
hear a black cat scuttle after a rat.
A trash can stands in front of a VW bus,
and waterbugs hover near water.
But these things are incidental—
what is central is the man, unable
to help himself get up, or stumble home
or someplace else,

and three windows in a Burmese factory,
with a blaze of light emanating out,
and the regular rhythms of a loom at work,
and a hundred and forty workers
on their knees, giving a midnight
blessing for the moon, and then them all,
going back to sewing silk dresses and
cotton pants for the readers of my poems.

PARKING GARAGE

We see them down below us,
in the orange glow of a parking garage.
Two figures lost in shade, some nameless cars
edged in tight against the curb.
One man casts his cumbersome shadow out
away from the cluster of darkened vehicles.
The other, bent over one of the silvery bodies,
flashes a quart of half-spent spirits.
Perhaps that's what they're doing now,
giving names to the living things around them.
Talking over slow runners at Aqueduct,
the mud slides of Vesuvius, or how black holes
will feed our feeling of emptiness.
Maybe they're re-naming the cars and the scotch
and the overpowering smells of gasoline.
What will they call the numbers of the jobless,
and the moons which orbit around Uranus?
They hang around and bless the waste and grandeur
of cities like this, and seek out the divine
in the shrunken, tired, worn-out things.
No one emerges from the pale elevator doors,

or strolls in for his Cadillac or Montecarlo.
It must be way past midnight.
One of them leans into a gathering breeze,
staring down at fine raindrops on cement.
You can hear a car start, deep
inside the mouth of the parking garage.
A woman's silhouette crosses the green-lit
door of the service entrance.
The men won't leave until everything is said
and done, and secretly, I wish I could be a part
of this, but from up here, I can't see what
they see: let's leave it to them,
they do it beautifully.

IV   THE MAN ON THE MOON

DEPARTURE

for Anselm Kiefer

The straw and iron
of open fields, and coal, and dust
and soldier's lives.
A cow calving at dawn, the thrown-off
clothes of two girls in love.
Under the earth lie many men,
bent and crumpled into collapsed foxholes
and streams of living cesspools.
The Americans dig trenches, practice
filling in these pits of death
for the next onslaught,
while the curl of the fern turns inward
under the rust-colored corn,
the archaeologist's wooden staff
plugging up all the holes.
The god above is the god within,
cries Aaron, as prairie wolves
devour the slain bull.
Where is the valley of the dry bones?

A pillar of clouds majestically rises,
shepherds returning to their flocks,
as a huge red eye circles
the mountains and blinks
the morning into afternoon.

WILLOW

When I see these trees weeping,
their arms spread out for me to sleep
beneath, the memory of her
floods back, and we walk the high rock
cliffs again, hunt for copperheads,
chase away the neighbors' cats
and scare the crows that eat the corn.
I walk alone by the river's edge,
under the Baldwin Bridge which separates
the continents, drink out of wine
flasks abandoned by the tides, kneel down
beside and contemplate the oozing
condoms strewn along the beach, and know
they are a part of me, at least
what people wanted me to be.
On bikes we'd tyrannize the Deans,
who lived together in a shack
and drove the taxis for the town.
Once they chased us, driving a fender
straight into my back tire,
and I saw the end, and, luckily,

the hedge which broke my fall.
I stand, too, in the locker room nude,
a towel before my skinny hips, the boys
with pubic hair and man-sized cocks
jeering at the rest of us.
And I hear the motorcyclist,
speeding around the bend,
wrenching the brake handle, skidding
over himself and the collie
in his path, the mess of blood
and leaves and fur, spilling in the road.
Willow limps home, sidelong in the dark,
with her dark mother's eyes
no longer on fire, to her nine pups
waiting, and me, thirteen,
holding a glass of chocolate milk.
A back leg severed, her spine broken
in two, the beautiful Egyptian eyes
looking only inward now. I kept
hoping the rider was crippled for life,
spitting up blood, or trembling
before God in purgatory, as we sat
in a small green room and they fed
her shivering body into a cold machine.
Something clamped down hard, stank
of electric trains. Unable to cry,
I thought of the gas chambers,
somehow purified. My head hurt,
I couldn't hear my mother's words,
the pain drew into me and a rock took root.
A week later, my parents splitting up
for good, I boarded a bus for seminary

school, deep in the Connecticut woods,
far from everything I ever knew.
We learned to speak Spanish and think
like Chairman Mao, we looked at Goya's
etchings, saw the men strung up
yet somehow smiling till the end, that wry
ironical grin of those who know
and will not say. And every dawn
we'd pray for health and bread, but
I couldn't join the choruses aloud,
Thy kingdom come, thy will be done,
on earth as it is in heaven.
And every night I'd cry myself to sleep,
and plead to God to have my dog again,
her company to keep. Once, I dug
in the leaves until a soft underbelly
found its way into my frozen fingers.
It shivered, too, as if out of glass,
blinking its great red ball-peen eye.
One of its feet was smashed and mangled
into bits: I wondered if this salamander
might have been a mother, too.
Here in the woods, far from stores
and the odors of girls at mirrors,
we learned to wrestle, receive the fist
without flinching. We taught ourselves
to masturbate alone, and feel the shame,
and hide our passions deep inside.
I'd walk for miles above Bull Mountain,
searching out spiders and the bluebird's
nesting place. We played lacrosse
and broke each other's legs, learned

incantatory spells from **Mrs.** Chandler's
ghost who murdered those who told the truth.
Secretly we kissed and shared our hog-
nosed snakes, raked the fields and ran
in packs with burning stakes. Cicadas
calmed the winds and seed pods flew
to far-off lands, Ho Chi Minh City,
or, perhaps, the Philippines. There were
no dogs for me to love, and mourning doves
would take me up the stairs each night,
to the vast sleeping halls, and the lack
of light, the same old songs of war
they sang up there at night. And there
in bed, I travelled to the willow tree,
to visit her who always slept with me.
And every Eucharist he puts the wafer
on my tongue and sets firm hands upon
my head, and as the bread disintegrates,
I think of those trees, still weeping.

ON THE SAMSON

We sat at the stern of a dry-docked tug,
lights of the city rising across the river.
You kept going on about fear, cast in the soul,
and the invasion of Santo Domingo.
I kept drinking beer, watched the kingfishers
plunging into the frozen moonlit waters.
Trains in the ConRail yard screeched
as they buckled clumsily into each other.
Homo sapiens with humanistic tendencies,
you kept calling our race of men.

The stars were the ones for all the world.
In the narrow berth of the cabin,
you took me like a child and opened me.
Como un flor, you said,
as we drifted off to sleep.

DEAD COMMUNISTS IN THEIR COFFINS, 1871

Seven of them, set upright
in pine boxes with beards unwashed
and jet black hair, genitals
exposed and swelling in the sun.
Arms cross over skinny chests,
plugged up with tiny gunshot wounds
and bits of animal hair that seem
to come from somewhere else.
The dark bruises on shoulders and hips
betray the counter-revolution:
dragged through whetstone streets
and barbed-wire lots, the weight
of these bodies has been lifted away.
Why are they smiling or looking up,
and where are all of their clothes?
Apostles of labor, set out to be seen,
identified, then chucked with the rest
into mass graves behind the palace.
People are eating rat pies again,
leaving their scraps in the alleys,

74

waiting for generals to lacerate
the legs of fools and prisoners,
to teach somebody a lesson, pay
the price and bring back order,
set the lines for bread and water.
Behind the men, a row of silhouettes
suggests the stables of Versailles,
while under their feet the pungent soil
turns in on itself in regular, plowed
furrows which once were for corn.
The ruins of a fort, perhaps, amidst
the sand and straw of yellow fields.
The bricklayer's mud-caked mouth
breaks open with a last cry as his
second daughter pushes her way out
of the womb without him.
A tailor lies cramped in a too-small
box, quiet and unconcerned, having
lost his shop and rented room
in a fire the week before.
Two weavers touch fingertips across
the flimsy boards, together now
as they were in work and love, and
another crouches between planks
laid out for a circus giantess.
The long thin back of the journalist
is twisted, as if a rod or shell
still agonized the vertebra.
The last, younger than the rest,
holds a crushed felt hat over his loins,
still shy and virginal, staring out
at me as if to say

we lived for you,
for you the lost loves burned and the bones
cracked over horse carts and the hot coals,
for you we worked at Lenin and Bakunin,
to make the world more safe,
we lived for you,
and he seems to ask if anything
at all has changed, as I stand before
his image and watch him shiver there.

MEMORY OF AMMENHAUSEN

Was wirst du tun, Gott, wenn ich sterbe?
R. M. RILKE

In this Hessian village, church bells pealed
and pealed until one broke loose from its halter.
What was happening? Another war was over.
Farmers, milkmaids, women from the paper mill
danced in the streets which flowed in blood and gold.
Everyone was crying or laughing violently.
It was over, My God, it was over.
Only one woman kept a straight face, a dark-haired mother
who breast-fed other women's children.
Three of her men were dead, lost somewhere
beyond the grave.
Some of the stones were marked with daffodils,
others with broken sticks. She was the pillar of salt
that no one turned around to look at.

ON A PAINTING BY PICOT

It was like this the first night
that we were together—you lay like Psyche
upon the hardwood bed, and me,
scratched by my own arrow, unable to leave
though my plane would fly in less than an hour.
When I saw this painting in the Louvre,
everything came back to me, the softness of your skin,
how smooth were your breasts that did not rise
with every breath, the crimson curtains
and behind the marble wall where we slept,
I imagined Carpathian hills and olive trees,
the sheep bleating and the tiny brook
that I had seen you swimming in.
But this was not Arcadia, but Kassel, Germany,
after the second war, and the buildings bore
the scars of far angrier gods than Venus,
our jealous arbiter of love. Yet I saw your hand
lay out the bed to call me back, my wings
still not shaken out and all my prowess
shrivelled like a boy's from cold.
As you slept the silken wraps slipped from around

your hips, full and cool and fleshy,
a perfect Lucas Cranach goddess of the sea.
You whispered in your sleep to me,
Take us down by the river to Prosperine,
and I will prove my love,
but Venus wouldn't let me take you.
I didn't want to wake you. So I packed my things
and left some cigarettes, a note which said
we might meet somewhere else, long after
your sisters had thrown themselves upon the rocks,
after you'd made the world a better place
with your beauty and your art, stronger than that
which we might have had together. And then
I flew away, knowing we'd meet again some day!

ROLAND C. NICKERSON
STATE PARK

We started out on bikes
from Waquoit Bay, where Wampanoags
used to fish for flounder.
Somebody took a picture of us:
shorts, rude smiles, Alpine hats.
I remember the gluey smell of the pines,
and starlings, clustered, black
in spirit as the clouds
which hid the summer sun.
Huge gypsy moths spread out
their cottony wombs across the boughs
of scrub oak trees.
We had on backpacks and rain gear,
pedaled hard through drizzle,
pushing ourselves away
from the chains of family.
It was just a two-day trip, up
the backside of Cape Cod,
but we felt like frenzied Sherpas
making our way to the highest peak.

We were together by default,
uprooted from our regular worlds
by parents with waking lives.
We'd walk in the birches,
searching out beaver dams
or shooting cans full of BBs.
He had a younger sister
with a horse, which once with its
yellowed teeth tried to bite
off my hand along with a bitter root.
We passed a fairgrounds, closed down
by bad weather, but I was sure
I saw a camel, peeking its forlorn muzzle
out of a bedraggled circus tent.

We passed a mansion, too, set back
into the trees of a Jesuit monastery.
A rainbow stretched the length of sky,
as if angels were departing.
Beyond a driving range, Stewie
got a flat, and we hitched a ride
to the nearest filling station.
As we waited for the man to fix the tire,
he showed us pictures of nude women
with huge pink breasts and small dark slits
hung up over the carburetor bench.
He gave us black coffee, told us he knew
where we were going, that soon the rain
would clear and we would be free to leave.
He said that he knew a short cut
to the forest, that he had a special
Swedish cooking stove, that he would show
us the only way to go.

Deep in a grove of sycamores,
he helped us with the two-man tent.
Across the lake from Winnebagos, *here,*
he said, we would be safe and sound.
He helped us to light the fire,
cook the bacon and potatoes, wash the dishes
afterwards, coloring the flames with salt.
He told ghost stories and fairy tales,
said it was then too late to go back to town.
There wasn't a single noise in the forest.
Until I heard his heavy breathing in the tent,
soft tuckings and rufflings of down.
I almost laughed out loud—this
was too predictable!
And then he took my hand in his, delicately
brought it to his side.

I knew what was happening, what might
happen next, and I pretended I wasn't there.
A fear gripped me, but also a perfect
objectivity, as if I was floating above us.
I felt the thing limp in my palm,
start to grow and rise and pump like a heart.
He was gentle, something only now
I recognize—I was scared and thought
of dying, descending from that sombre night
into some unknown and fiery moonscape.
I thought of Hieronymous Bosch,
how I never understood why they called it
a garden of *delights,* images of people
burning upside down or being crushed
by insects or elephants or mice.

I saw myself there, in a glass-covered egg,
twisted into a ball and bleeding
on my brother. I closed my eyes, tight
as a fault in the earth, shutting
up its mouth of flame.

Gathering my strength, I pushed him off
just once—and he rolled over
towards the other side of the tent.
Oh no! Not Stewart! And I saw myself
at the graveside of my friend, dropping
petals of dogwood down into the hole.
I heard a harsh panting, and scratchings
on cloth, and then, the small internal cry
of a bird, muffled in a sleeping bag.
All night, I stayed awake and couldn't move
and listened for every breath of the forest.
Near dawn, a clumsy animal was sniffing
at the ashes, licking at scraps of beef,
and I imagined a behemoth grizzly bear,
come to wipe us out for all our sins.
I welcomed the imminent crash and swipe
of his giant paws that would end this night
of terror, but instead, some sparrows woke
and a light poked into a corner of the tent.
Once there was day, I ran out to the lake,
shed my clothes and plunged in deep.
Paddling like a Labrador, I felt
every part of my naked, unbruised body
and washed myself completely of his touch.
I touched myself in every place, my heart
still pounding, thankful that I was whole.

I felt unimaginably great.
As I swam, I felt a heaviness slip off,
float down towards the darkness underneath,
as if a massive skin of snake had left me
forever. When I came out, I lit a fire
and sank into its reverie.
When they got up, one at a time, I pretended
that nothing had happened, still afraid
he might be a murderer, waiting for
the perfect moment.
I don't remember anything else, how we got
back to town or whether we continued the trip.
I never spoke of this to anyone, until many
years later I lay in the arms of one I loved,
and I cried and cried for what that man
had taken from me, and for what I shed
that dawn into the bottomless lake of the park.

RUSTAM AND RAKSH

(The famous Persian hero, son of Zal, and his horse)

He lay lifeless, in a dark cellarway
full of spider webs and thin black corners
for the brown bats.
One eye cracked open, the heart
had ceased to tremble.
A huge cold cavern underground, walls lined
with lime and amber glass, long lists
of banned books, wild petrified eggs.
We would go down to stock up on things,
but then the beautiful Moushka was missing,
and the Kurds came to investigate,
digging wide trenches into the mud floor.
Murders were common in this neighborhood,
and this one was somehow connected
to Lefty with the one bad eye,
a Burmese from Chinatown.
People swarmed into the damp basement
to help them dig, sweat, root out the mystery.
Water rained down from leaking pipes,

out of the gutters and the billowing sky.
Pig-like antelopes, some sort of primordial
aardvarks, assisted with the dredging,
using their vacuum snouts as ballast
for the tricky operations.
A field full of peasants harvesting rice,
prisoners gouging out unnecessary holes.
I was watching, a few of the giant pigs
on each side of me, their long strands
of genital hair matted and clinging
to my shivering arms.
The body was gone. But a shovel struck
a thick skin, the carcass of a stallion
crusted over in filth and stiff from death.
The darkness grew as the slogging noises
became unbearable. When a small, ordinary bird
flew in to sing, some of the light returned,
and we knew it was the horse, Raksh.

THE MAN ON THE MOON

Outside, the crickets sounded like coquis,
and the huge orange globe hung over the swamps,
the mystical lady of El Yunque.
The Roman poets called her Cynthia, and Hardy,
the dark mistress of melancholy.
But here in Florida, she was made of green cheese,
and seen to be a man on top of that.
I had confused the lunar caves with cratered forests
near Saigon, the dusty plains with the Bay of Pigs,
the bloodied soldiers with long-leaping robots.
It was the night I showed Mark how to make love,
the way the grown-ups did, his small hand moving
along mine, our lips passing over the soft flesh,
the coming to know our boys' firm nipples.
We tried and tried to make it work, the boy
on the girl, the girl on the boy.
We couldn't be sure of the differences, of all
the imagined places, of what we had to do.
I felt his skin hot against mine, and the cool fan
blew a breeze across our gold convertible couch.
The kissing was marvelous, and so was the after-image
of the man, walking for the first time on the moon.

CATHEDRAL OF THE PINES

The altar overlooked Mt. Washington.
All down the slopes to the cliff,
a bed of long red needles.
The underlying rock was shale and basalt.
No one around but a grandmother, the caretaker.
But an organ was playing,
strangely resonant in this coniferous hall
where the wind was picking up
and carrying off the whiffs of resin.
Cold? A little, for July,
and the ghosts of the homeless
took up all the tree-trunk benches.
I could have stayed out there all day,
listening to *Trees,* lugubriously played
and the choral refrains from nasty jays
forever goading each other into action.
The music went out into the hillsides.
So did the ghosts, when the mass was over.

ABOUT THE AUTHOR

William Allen has an M.A. in History and in English from New York University, where he has taught creative writing. He has also taught in the Dominican Republic and District 65/UAW in New York City. He has worked with the artists of Group Material, and with Artists Call Against U.S. Intervention in Central America. He was awarded a D.A.A.D. grant to go to Germany for writing and translating poetry. He is the winner, along with the fiction writer Agnes Rossi, of the 1986 publication prize of the Creative Writing Department of New York University. The judge was Philip Levine.